Your Rights as a U.S. Citizen

ROB MAURY

WE CAME TO AMERICA

MASON CREST PUBLISHERS • PHILADELPHIA

In September 1984, nearly 10,000 people participated in one of the largest naturalization ceremonies in U.S. history at the Orange Bowl Stadium in Miami. Naturalization is the final step immigrants must take to become citizens of the United States.

Your Rights as a U.S. Citizen

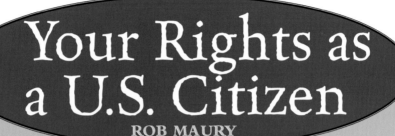

ROB MAURY

WE CAME TO AMERICA

MASON CREST PUBLISHERS • PHILADELPHIA

Mason Crest Publishers
370 Reed Road
Broomall PA 19008
www.masoncrest.com

First printing

1 3 5 7 9 8 6 4 2

Library of Congress Cataloging-in-Publication Data
on file at the Library of Congress

ISBN 1-59084-105-0

Table of Contents

WE CAME TO AMERICA

America's Ethnic Heritage

Barry Moreno, librarian

Statue of Liberty/

Ellis Island National Monument

Ethnic diversity is one of the most striking characteristics of the American identity. In the United States the Bureau of the Census officially recognizes 122 different ethnic groups. North America's population had grown by leaps and bounds, starting with the American Indian tribes and nations—the continent's original people—and increasing with the arrival of the European colonial migrants who came to these shores during the 16th and 17th centuries. Since then, millions of immigrants have come to America from every corner of the world.

But the passage of generations and the great distance of America from the "Old World"—Europe, Africa, and Asia—has in some cases separated immigrant peoples from their roots. The struggle to succeed in America made it easy to forget past traditions. Further, the American spirit of freedom, individualism, and equality gave Americans a perspective quite different from the view of life shared by residents of the Old World.

Immigrants of the 19th and 20th centuries recognized this at once. Many tried to "Americanize" themselves by tossing away their peasant clothes and dressing American-style even before reaching their new homes in the cities or the countryside of America. It was not so easy to become part of America's culture, however. For many immigrants, learning English was quite a hurdle. In fact, most older immigrants clung to the old ways, preferring to speak their native languages and follow their familiar customs and traditions. This was easy to do when ethnic neighborhoods abounded in large North American cities like New York, Montreal, Philadelphia, Chicago, Toronto, Boston, Cleveland, St. Louis, New Orleans and San Francisco. In rural areas, farm families—many of them Scandinavian, German, or Czech—established their own tightly knit communities. Thus foreign languages and dialects, religious beliefs, Old World customs, and certain class distinctions flourished.

The most striking changes occurred among the children of immigrants, whose hopes and dreams were different from those of their parents. They began breaking away from the Old World customs, perhaps as a reaction to the embarrassment of being labeled "foreigner." They badly wanted to be Americans, and assimilated more easily than their parents and grandparents. They learned to speak English without a foreign accent, to dress and act like other Americans. The assimilation of the children of immigrants was encouraged by social contact—games, schools, jobs, and military service—which further broke down the barriers between immigrant groups and hastened the process of Americanization. Along the way, many family traditions were lost or abandoned.

Today, the pride that Americans have in their ethnic roots is one of the abiding strengths of both the United States and Canada. It shows that the theory which called America a "melting pot" of the world's people was never really true. The thought that a single "American" would emerge from the combination of these peoples has never happened, for Americans have grown more reluctant than ever before to forget the struggles of their ethnic forefathers. The growth of cultural studies and genealogical research indicates that Americans are anxious not to entirely lose this identity, whether it is English, French, Chinese, African, Mexican, or some other group. There is an interest in tracing back the family line as far as records or memory will take them. In a sense, this has made Americans a divided people; proud to be Americans, but proud also of their ethnic roots.

As a result, many Americans have welcomed a new identity, that of the hyphenated American. This unique description has grown in usage over the years and continues to grow as more Americans recognize the importance of family heritage. In the end, this is an appreciation of America's great cultural heritage and its richness of its variety.

Personal Stories of
United States Immigration

Many people come to America looking for a better life, but not every person's experiences are pleasant.

In 1977, Donna was 13 and swimming in the waters surrounding her island home, Jamaica. Life was warm under the tropical sun, and Donna played on the beach with her two brothers, ages 15 and three. She went to school like most kids her age. However, not many kids could pick and eat mangos off a tree on their way home. One morning, her mother woke her up, saying, "Get dressed. We're leaving for America."

Donna's parents wanted freedom from political *persecution*. Jamaica's newly appointed prime minister had *allied* himself with Cuba's Communist leader Fidel Castro. That morning, Donna and her family boarded a plane headed for Miami, Florida, with one suitcase each and $50. They were lucky because many people didn't make it past the airport guards. Donna and her family had to pretend they were only leaving to visit America.

President George W. Bush poses with new American citizens after a swearing-in ceremony on Ellis Island. One of the president's goals is to reform the Immigration and Naturalization Service.

In Miami, Donna and her brothers stayed with friends while her parents went further north to Baltimore, Maryland. Terrified of being sent back to Jamaica, Donna and her brothers stayed inside. The carefree girl who once skipped on the wide, open beach now felt trapped, frightened, and alone.

Once her parents were settled and employed, they sent for the children. For the second time in her life, Donna hopped on a plane headed for a place unknown to her. When she landed in Baltimore, it was the middle of winter—a winter with heavy snowfall. Wearing sandals and no coats, Donna and her brothers were not prepared for the freezing temperatures of the Baltimore winters. Living with snow was something that had never occurred to Donna. She was used to tropical weather and sandy beaches.

Immigrants have come to the United States for many reasons. Some wish to escape religious or political persecution in their homelands. In the past 40 years, for example, many people have fled Cuba because of the policies of dictator Fidel Castro, pictured here waving the Cuban flag at a rally.

Donna's parents had found a place for her and her brothers to live, but it wasn't with them. For three months, the children lived in one room in a townhouse in downtown Baltimore. Scared, Donna anxiously waited for the day her family would be together again. The only thing

GLORIA ESTEFAN

Most immigrants come to the United States seeking the "American Dream," and Gloria Estefan was no different. Gloria Fajardo (Estefan is her married name) was born in Havana, Cuba, in 1957. Fidel Castro's policies forced Gloria and her family to migrate to the United States in 1959. Her father served with the United States Army as a soldier in Vietnam. After Vietnam, he developed *multiple sclerosis*. As the oldest daughter, Gloria took care of him and her younger sister while her mother worked to support the family. Her music career was launched while she attended the University of Miami. There she joined a band called The Miami Sound Machine. Since then, she has won many awards, including several Grammys. In addition to continuing her successful music career she is also an outspoken supporter of a free Cuba.

available for Donna and her older brother to do was take care of their younger brother.

The day finally came when Donna's family was together again. For the third time in less than a year, her life changed once more. She was now living in Baltimore, going to an American school, and dreaming of her former tropical-paradise home.

Years later, her parents decided to become **naturalized** United States citizens. Today, they raise foster children as a way to say thanks to the country that fostered their children. After becoming a

It was hard for Donna to leave Jamaica, because the island country is beautiful and warm. However, most people in Jamaica are poor, and immigrants have a better chance at a good life in America.

naturalized United States citizen, her older brother joined the United States Marine Corps. Her younger brother is going to college.

Donna's decision to become a naturalized American citizen didn't come as easy for her as it had for her parents. She was an adult when her parents became citizens, leaving it up to her to decide if she wanted to give up her Jamaican citizenship. She still dreamed of her tropical-paradise home. Today, she still lives in Baltimore, but now with her husband and three young children. It was having children that made her decide to become a United States citizen. They represented the first generation of Jamaican-American, natural-born United States citizens in Donna's family. As the only member of her family not a United States citizen, being sent back to Jamaica finally became a real terror for her.

The test wasn't as hard for her as it might have been for other immigrants because Donna had spent all her high school years in the United States. It did take years, however, to get through each step leading up to the day she finally took the oath.

Citizenship has proven to be beneficial. Now Donna can help determine what happens in her community, her children's schools, and who represents her in government by voting. She can visit Jamaica, lie on its sunny beaches, and swim in its blue water without fear of having to immediately leave with only a suitcase and $50. ✺

HAKEEM OLAJUWON

Hakeem Olajuwon's coming-to-America story started on the basketball court. He was born in 1963 in Lagos, Nigeria. As a boy, he went to school (where he learned French and four dialects of the Nigerian language) and loved to play soccer and handball. As a teen, he started playing basketball. Within weeks, thanks to his height and skill, he made the Nigerian national team. An American coach

traveling in Nigeria was so overwhelmed by his talent that he searched for a college in the United States that would offer Hakeem a scholarship.

Hakeem came to the United States for a college education and a chance to play basketball at the University of Houston. He remembers his first stop in the United States as being very cold. His first stop, like many coming to the United States, was in New York.

Hakeem's decision to become a United States citizen in 1993 was a difficult one. However, he felt a debt of gratitude to the country that had given so much to him, including an education, a career as a professional basketball player, and a family.

History of United States Immigration

The United States started as a nation of immigrants, and throughout the centuries the nation has grown and developed because of immigrants. Most immigrants come to the United States for the chance to find better jobs with better pay, thus paving the way for a better life for their families. Groups of immigrants have also come here looking for religious or political freedom. Political freedom was so important to Donna's parents that they gave up everything they had to achieve it.

In many cities in the United States, it is possible to drive from one end of the city to the other and pass many neighborhoods that embrace a culture from another country. All those culturally enhanced neighborhoods existing together in one city are what make this country a diverse and unique community.

Immigration to the United States started about 25,000 B.C. with the Native Americans. The world had just come out of the last Ice Age, and

> More than 12 million immigrants passed through Ellis Island before the station was closed in 1954. Today, the descendants of those processed at Ellis Island number more than 100 million. The buildings have been turned into a museum of immigration history, where visitors to the island can learn about the immigration experience.

the glacial ice at the North Pole lowered sea levels, thereby exposing a land bridge from Asia to North America. Following migrating herds, people from Asia walked over this land bridge and into Alaska. They eventually spread throughout present-day Canada, the United States, Mexico, and down into South America.

It is believed the second significant migration to America was around A.D. 1000 when Viking explorer Leif Eriksson sailed across the Atlantic and landed on Canada's east coast. However, Europeans did not begin to settle in North America until after Christopher Columbus landed there in 1492. Columbus had been looking for a westward route to Asia, but actually sailed into the Caribbean. During Columbus's life, he made four voyages in which he discovered and named most of the islands we now call the West Indies and sailed along much of South America's east coast. Although Columbus never admitted that he had not found Asia, another explorer named Amerigo Vespucci declared that a "New World" had been found after he explored Brazil's east coast in 1501. The discovery of this New World launched a major migration of Europeans into America, known as the Colonial period.

During the 1520s and 1530s, the Spanish made several attempts to settle in North America. In 1565, Spain established the first permanent European colony in North America at St. Augustine, Florida. By 1598, Spanish settlers had moved as far west as New Mexico.

The French moved north through America and into present-day Canada, settling in Acadia (Nova Scotia) in 1604 and Quebec in 1608.

Viking sailors make the voyage across the Atlantic between Europe and America. Vikings were thought to have landed in North America around A.D. 1000, but never attempted colonization because of hostile natives.

Settlers trade with Indians at Jamestown, the first permanent English settlement in North America. While some settlers attempted to keep peaceful relations with the native Americans, this would prove to be difficult to maintain.

From there, they moved south into central North America, establishing New Orleans, Louisiana in 1718.

In 1606, three English ships landed in present-day Virginia. A year later, the first permanent English colony, Jamestown, was founded. Other English settlements would soon follow. The Pilgrims left England searching for religious freedom. In 1620, they crossed the Atlantic on the *Mayflower* and founded the Plymouth colony in New England. A few years later the Puritans, a religious group that valued hard work, success, and education, settled on the shores of Massachusetts Bay. In 1682, William Penn founded the colony of Pennsylvania, which was open to settlers of all religious beliefs.

The Swedish established New Sweden in 1638 in present-day Delaware. The Dutch founded the New Netherlands colony in 1614, and within it grew the town of New Amsterdam in 1626. In 1654, a group of Jewish settlers arrived at New Amsterdam. The Dutch eventually gained control of New Sweden. Later, the English took over the Dutch colony, renaming the city New York.

The African migration was a migration unlike any other. Africans were kidnapped from their homes and forced to work and live in North America. It is believed that the first slaves were sold on the continent of North America in 1619 to settlers at Jamestown. Prior to that, Portuguese sailors had brought slaves to the Spanish colonies in the Caribbean. Some Europeans came to America as **indentured** servants. Unlike the slaves, however, indentured servants could gain their freedom after they had worked for their masters for a set period of time, usually seven years.

After the Revolutionary War ended in 1783, a new nation was born with a population of two and a half million people. Diversity was already the American way. During the 1780s, thousands of Scottish immigrants arrived in America. Ten years later, thousands of French

23

STATUE OF LIBERTY

The Statue of Liberty (left) greeted many immigrants coming across the Atlantic Ocean in the early 1900s. The Statue of Liberty was a gift of friendship from France. Since 1886, Lady Liberty has stood tall (151 feet tall) on Liberty Island in New York Harbor near Ellis Island. In her right hand she holds high a torch representing liberty, and in her left a tablet with the date July 4, 1776 inscribed on it in roman numerals. The seven spikes of her crown represent the seven seas and the seven continents. There are 25 windows symbolizing the 25 gemstones of the earth. On the base of the statue is the poem "The New Colossus" by Emma Lazarus:

> Not like the brazen giant of Greek fame
>
> With conquering limbs astride from land to land
>
> Here at our sea-washed, sunset gates shall stand
>
> A mighty woman with a torch, whose flame
>
> Is the imprisoned lightning, and her name
>
> Mother of Exiles. From her beacon-hand
>
> Glows worldwide welcome; her mild eyes command
>
> The air-bridged harbor that twin cities frame.
>
> "Give me your tired, your poor,
>
> Your huddled masses yearning to breathe free;
>
> The wretched refuse of your teeming shore,
>
> Send these, the homeless, tempest-tossed to me
>
> I lift my lamp beside the golden door!"

The Statue of Liberty became a national monument symbolizing freedom in 1924.

people who opposed the bloody excesses of the French Revolution came to America seeking freedom.

In 1790, Congress passed an act requiring a two-year residency before immigrants could qualify for citizenship. Five years later, Congress raised the time period to five years. Then, in 1798, Congress raised it to 14 years with the passage of the Alien and Sedition Acts.

During the 1840s, years of potato *famine* forced many Irish to leave their homes for the United States. Starting in 1840, the next 37 years saw 37 million people arrive in America. During this period, Scandinavian, eastern European, and Italian immigrants began arriving in large numbers. Due to political reasons, in 1848 many Germans found their way across the Atlantic as well. Chinese immigrants begin arriving on the West Coast during the California Gold Rush that same year.

American employers had been paying for Chinese immigrants' passage to the United States in exchange for cheap labor. In 1882, Congress halted immigration from China by passing the Chinese Exclusion Act. Other laws passed denied the immigration of criminals, people with diseases, and people likely to be dependent on public assistance. The Alien Contract Labor Laws of 1885 prohibited immigrants from entering the country to work under contracts made before they arrived. Exceptions were made for entertainers, educators, ministers, servants, and some skilled workers.

In 1891, Congress created the Immigration and Naturalization Service (INS) to administer federal laws relating to the admission, exclusion, and *deportation* of immigrants. The Immigration and Naturalization

ELLIS ISLAND

In the first half of the 20th century, immigrants coming from European countries first had to pass through Ellis Island before entering the United States. In 1892, Ellis Island (named for Samuel Ellis, a New York City merchant who had owned the island in the late 1700s) served as the headquarters for United States Immigration and Naturalization Service after the Castle Garden building in Manhattan became unable to handle the number of immigrants coming into the country. It is estimated that approximately 12 million immigrants passed through the island during the time it was open. Ellis Island was closed in 1954 due to a decrease in immigration. In 1965, the island was turned over to the National Park Service. In 1990, after six years of renovations, Ellis Island was turned into a museum chronicling four centuries of United States immigration. It is estimated that nearly one out of every three Americans has a relative who passed through the Island.

Service was also given the duty of lawfully naturalizing immigrants. The gateway to America, Ellis Island in New York Harbor, opened in 1892 and served as the Immigration and Naturalization Service's immigrant-screening station until it was closed in 1954.

From 1900 to the 1920s, about 10 million people immigrated to the United States. Japanese immigrants were the largest group settling in the Pacific Northwest. In 1907, the United States made an agreement with Japan that Japan would deny passports to Japanese workers trying to leave for the United States. In return, the United

During the 1920s, a series of laws restricted immigration to the United States. This political cartoon from 1921 shows Uncle Sam slowing the rush of European immigrants to a trickle.

States wouldn't enact laws denying Japanese immigrants entry. The Immigration Act of 1917 limited the areas of the world from which people were allowed to immigrate, and literacy, moral, mental, physical, and economic standards were set. In 1921, Congress enacted a *quota* system, limiting the number of immigrants allowed in the country each year. In 1924, Congress passed another immigration act, dropping the number of immigrants allowed each year even further.

The Immigration Act of 1924 and the Great Depression during the 1930s reduced immigration drastically. In 1941, Congress lowered the immigration numbers further by not allowing entry to anyone whose presence might endanger public safety.

It wasn't until 1943 that Congress started to lift immigration *bans* by allowing 105 Chinese immigrants into the country a year. The War Brides Act of 1945 allowed entry to foreign women who had married U.S.

soldiers or sailors serving overseas during World War II. The Displaced Persons Acts of 1948 and 1950, as well as the Refugee Relief Act of 1953, ushered in half a million people escaping the devastation of Europe or Communist persecution. Also in the 1950s, Mexican immigration numbers rose as people there fled poverty and a strict *dictatorship*. In 1965, all existing immigration laws were combined into the Immigration and Nationality Act. The Act made possible for people from all countries to have equal immigration opportunities.

The Immigration and Nationality Act of 1965 set the limit of immigrants from the Eastern Hemisphere at 170,000 and 120,000 from the Western Hemisphere. In 1978, separate limits were done away with and a worldwide limit of 290,000 immigrant *visas*, with a maximum of 20,000 for each country, was set by an amendment to the act. The Refugee Act of 1980 reduced the worldwide quota to 270,000 and established a limit of 50,000 for refugees.

The Immigration Reform and Control Act of 1986 took aim at illegal immigration by penalizing employers hiring illegal immigrants. The Immigration Act of 1990 established a limit of 700,000 immigrants for the next three years and 675,000 after that. In 1996, Congress made it easier to deport illegal immigrants by passing the Illegal Immigrant Reform and Immigration Responsibility Act.

More recently, in the year 2001, the Child Citizenship Act gave citizenship to children born outside of the United States who have at least one citizen as a parent. ✺

We the People

of the United States, in order to form a more perfect Union, establish Justice, insure domestic Tranquility, provide for the common defence, promote the general Welfare, and secure the Blessings of Liberty to ourselves and our Posterity, do ordain and establish this Constitution for the United States of America.

Article I

Article II

Article III

Article IV

Article V

Article VI

Article VII

done in Convention by the Unanimous Consent of the States present the Seventeenth Day of September in the Year of our Lord one thousand seven hundred and Eighty seven and of the Independence of the United States of America the Twelfth.

In Witness whereof We have hereunto subscribed our Names.

Rights of United States Citizens

After Donna became a citizen of the United States, she gained all the rights and privileges of citizenship. The only difference is that naturalized citizens can not be elected vice president or president of the United States.

The right to vote is arguably the greatest privilege a naturalized citizen gains. A major reason for this is taxes. A non-citizen is required to pay taxes while living and working in the United States but is not allowed to vote to help decide what those taxes are used for.

The U.S. Constitution, the document which provides the system of government for the United States, has been in use for more than 200 years. It provides laws and guidelines for the government and explains the rights of U.S. citizens.

On July 4, 1776, the 13 English colonies in North America declared their independence as a new nation with the document we call the Declaration of Independence. After defeating the British forces during the War for Independence, the new country—the United States of America—was governed by the Articles of Confederation. However, this system of government did not work very well. In 1787, George Washington and other American leaders decided to create a new system of government.

31

The result of their work, the United States Constitution, went into effect on June 21, 1788.

The Constitution set up a government with three branches: the legislative, the executive, and the judicial. A complex system of checks and balances was installed to ensure that all branches had equal power. One example of the checks and balances system is that Congress (the House of Representatives and Senate) can't pass a law if the President vetoes, or rejects, the law or if the Supreme Court declares the law **unconstitutional**.

Article One of the Constitution deals with the legislative branch of the United States government—the House of Representatives and the Senate. This is the branch of government that is responsible for making the laws of the United States. Article One ensures that all citizens who pay taxes will have representation in government. A **census** is taken every 10 years to determine the population size of the country, states, cities, and counties. The number of representatives in the House of Representatives is determined by the population sizes.

Article Two discusses the executive branch—the president and vice president. The president's duties include ensuring that the nation's laws are enforced and acting as commander-in-chief of all United States military forces. If the president is unable to fulfill his duties, the vice president assumes these responsibilities.

Article Three covers the judicial branch—the Supreme Court. The Supreme Court's duties include reviewing lower court decisions on any law or any court case brought before them.

The United States Supreme Court building stands in Washington, D.C. The Supreme Court is made up of nine justices whose task is to interpret the U.S. Constitution as it relates to the laws of the land.

Article Four keeps all the states on equal grounds. Article Five sets the standards for *amending* the Constitution. Article Six proclaims the Constitution as the supreme law of the land. Article Seven states that the approval of nine states was needed for the Constitution to go into effect.

WASHINGTON, DISTRICT OF COLUMBIA

Named for George Washington and Christopher Columbus, Washington, D.C., was established as a federal territory in 1790 and became the new capital of the United States. Today, the city's population has grown to over half a million. The Home Rule Act of 1974 established local elections for the mayor and city council. However, the federal government still primarily governs Washington, D.C. In March 2000, city residents sought representation in Congress, but were denied by a panel of judges.

The Constitution was made so that it could be amended as needed. On September 25, 1789, Congress proposed 12 amendments, and on December 15, 1791, 10 went into effect. These amendments addressed concerns and lingering fears that people had about repressive government. The 10 amendments are called the Bill of Rights. They guarantee certain rights and privileges to all citizens of the United States.

The First Amendment guarantees the freedom of speech, press, and religion. This means that the government cannot prevent a person from speaking out, a newspaper from running an article critical of the government, or a person from worshipping as he or she chooses, as long as these things do not infringe on any other person's rights.

The Second Amendment gives citizens the right to bear arms. In other words, this amendment says that everyone has the right to own a gun. How and in what respect the Second Amendment addresses the issue of gun control is heavily debated today.

The Third Amendment bans the housing of members of the military in civilian homes. During the Revolutionary War, English troops took over the homes of civilians, thus prompting the passage of this amendment.

The Fourth Amendment prevents illegal search and seizures. This means the police can not search or take away a person's property without reasonable cause.

The Fifth Amendment protects a citizen's rights during a trial. No one will stand trial unless a reasonable accusation has been made. No one can be tried twice for the same crime. Avoiding *self-incrimination* is also a citizen's right. The Fifth Amendment also prevents the

This 1919 poster, which features the Statue of Liberty, proclaims the advantages of living in America. Coming to the United States offers immigrants a better chance to "earn more, learn more" and even "own a home."

government from taking anyone's property unless it is in the public's best interest and a fair value is given for it.

The Sixth Amendment guarantees a speedy and public trial. It also ensures that a citizen has the right to know the charges he or she is being tried for and has the opportunity to confront witnesses and accusers.

The Seventh Amendment guarantees the right to a jury in a federal civil trial. The Eighth Amendment protects citizens against excessive *bail*, fines, and cruel and unusual punishments.

The Ninth Amendment protects any rights a citizen may have that aren't specifically written in the Constitution. Television, video games, and the Internet, for example, were not around when the Constitution was written. The Ninth Amendment extends already-written rights to issues concerning such modern-day inventions until the need arises to create new amendments.

The Tenth Amendment is a form of checks and balances that the states have concerning the federal government. It gives any powers not assigned to the federal government to the states and their citizens.

Since the passage of the Bill of Rights, there have been 17 additional amendments. Not all of these amendments, however, concern the citizens themselves. The Eleventh Amendment (passed in 1795) protects the states from certain types of lawsuits. The Twelfth Amendment (1804) sends the election of the president to the House of Representatives if the citizens and the Electoral College cannot come to a decision. The Seventeenth Amendment (1913) addresses *vacancies* in the Senate. The Twentieth Amendment (1933) sets the time period

UNITED STATES CONSTITUTION

For more than 200 years, the Constitution of the United States has been the supreme law of the country. It was written in 1787 at the Constitutional Convention in Philadelphia. The meeting was headed by George Washington and attended by 55 delegates representing 12 states (Rhode Island didn't send delegates). The first United States Congress added 12 amendments, but only 10 were agreed upon by the states. These 10 amendments are known today as the Bill of Rights. Besides George Washington, some other famous early Americans in attendance at the convention were Benjamin Franklin, James Madison, and Alexander Hamilton. Patrick Henry refused to attend, and Thomas Jefferson and John Adams were out of the country at the time. The original draft of the Constitution can be seen in the National Archives Building in Washington, D.C.

of a term of presidency and when Congressional sessions meet. The Twenty-second Amendment (1951) sets the number of terms for president at two (after Franklin D. Roosevelt was elected to four terms). The Twenty-fifth Amendment (1967) states that if the president resigns, the vice president takes office. And the Twenty-seventh Amendment (1992) addresses Congressional pay rates.

Certain other amendments deal directly with citizens' civil rights. The Thirteenth Amendment (1865) bans all slavery in the United States. The Fourteenth Amendment (1868) reinforces the Declaration of Independence's statement "that all men are created equal" by stating, "All persons born or naturalized in the United States...are citizens of the United States and the state wherein they reside." This

Visitors to the National Archives in Washington, D.C., look at original copies of the Declaration of Independence, the Constitution, and the Bill of Rights. These three documents are very important in American history, and great care is taken to make sure they are not damaged.

amendment also provides equal treatment to all citizens. The Fifteenth Amendment (1870) goes even further to say that no one can be denied the right to vote based on their race or on the fact that they were once slaves. The right to vote was extended to women with passage of the Nineteenth Amendment (1920). The Twenty-fourth Amendment (1964) restates that the right to vote is open to all citizens and addresses the issue of the *poll tax*. African Americans were being denied the right to vote unless they paid such a tax. The Twenty-sixth Amendment (1971) sets the voting age at 18.

38

The right to vote for the president of the United States is a basic American right, but it wasn't until the Twenty-third Amendment (1961) that residents of the District of Columbia were given this right.

Other amendments affect how citizens live. The Sixteenth Amendment (1913) allows Congress to impose an income tax. The Eighteenth Amendment (1919) started Prohibition, a ban on alcohol. It was later repealed by the Twenty-first Amendment (1933). ✳

DECLARATION OF INDEPENDENCE

It took Thomas Jefferson and a committee of colonial leaders from June 11 to June 28, 1776, to write the Declaration of Independence. When it was finished, they had created a document that expressed the feelings of a new nation—a nation that embraced the freedoms and liberties of the individual. The Declaration of Independence also expressed the nation's outrage against the King of England:

"He has obstructed the Administration of Justice

For imposing Taxes on us without our consent

For cutting off our Trade with all parts of the world

He has plundered our seas, ravaged our Coasts, burnt our towns, and

destroyed the lives of our people."

On July 4, 1776, such early Americans as John Hancock, Benjamin Franklin, John Adams, and Thomas Jefferson signed the Declaration of Independence. On that day, the United States of America was born. The original document can be seen in the rotunda of the National Archives Building in Washington, D.C.

Individuals take the Oath of Allegiance administered by a justice of the U.S. District Court at a swearing-in ceremony in September 1999. The oath states that the person reciting it renounces any allegiance to a foreign country or power. Once the oath has been taken, these immigrants will be American citizens.

The Naturalized Citizenship Process

Even though Donna's immigration story may be different from other immigrants, the process Donna went through to become a United States citizen is the same for everyone who comes to this country.

The first step an immigrant must take to gain U.S. citizenship is to get an Alien Registration Receipt Card (also called a green card). This allows an immigrant to work and live in the United States permanently while seeking citizenship. Green cards are usually obtained through the Diversity Visa Lottery, a program that was set up as part of the Immigration Act of 1990. The program is set up so that countries around the world do not continually receive **preferential** treatment year after year.

After five years, a permanent resident alien (an immigrant who wants to remain in the United States) can file for citizenship if certain requirements are met. These requirements include being at least 18 years of age (children under 18 become citizens when their parents are naturalized), having a good moral character (for example, they have been paying taxes and have not committed any crimes), an ability to read and write the English language (unless they are unable to do so for some physical reason, such as blindness), and having a knowledge of American history and its government. An accurate and complete application can help speed up the lengthy process.

WHY BECOME A CITIZEN?

What advantages does an immigrant gain from becoming a citizen? A naturalized citizen is given all the rights and privileges that a person born a citizen has, including the right to vote. A naturalized citizen can run for any public office except president and vice president. When a U.S. citizen travels to other countries, most only require a passport. A citizen may live outside the United States for as long as he or she wants; a green card only allows you to live outside the United States for a year. While in other countries, citizens can seek the help of United States embassies and consulates. Most civil service and law enforcement jobs require citizenship. Families of citizens can live in the United States with a permanent green card status. Citizens are also eligible for public assistance and are *immune* from deportation.

A citizenship test is given to determine the applicant's ability to read and write English and his or her knowledge of American history and government. The test consists of writing down on paper two **dictated** sentences, with at least one sentence written perfectly, and a knowledge test. The knowledge test can be given as an oral exam, but most people seeking citizenship prefer a multiple-choice test. A definite advantage to the multiple-choice test is being given a choice of answers. The test consists of 20 questions and takes about 30 minutes. Twelve correct answers are all that are needed to pass. Once the test is passed, the person's name and score is sent to the Immigration and Naturalization Service to continue the citizenship process. If someone fails the test, the

Immigration and Naturalization Service is not notified and that person is permitted to take the test again at no charge.

Some examples of the sentences that are dictated during the test are:

> Red, white, and blue are the colors of the American flag.
>
> The President lives in the White House.
>
> As a citizen, I will be able to vote.

Some examples of questions on the multiple-choice test are:

Which document starts with "We the people of the United States":

> A. Declaration of Independence
>
> B. Constitution
>
> C. Bill of Rights
>
> D. First Amendment

The first line in the National Anthem is:

> A. O say can you see
>
> B. My country 'tis of thee
>
> C. God Bless America
>
> D. America, America

Just like any other test, studying is an important part in being able to pass. Some suggested subjects to study are:

> The discovery and settlement of the original 13 colonies
>
> Information about the Revolutionary War, the founding of the United States and its independence
>
> The Declaration of Independence, Constitution and its Amendments, including the Bill of Rights
>
> The history of the westward expansion

Modern history (for example, women's rights, the Great
Depression, World War II, the civil rights movement)

Federal, state, and local government

United States symbols (for example, the American Flag, Statue
of Liberty, Liberty Bell, and Independence Hall)

After passing the test, a citizenship interview with an immigration officer is conducted. This interview may cover the person's reasons for coming to America and any questions needing to be answered about the application.

After completing the process, Donna finally received her immigration approval and the date for her naturalization ceremony. In a Baltimore courthouse, Donna's family watched her stand up and take the Oath of Allegiance to the United States of America:

Sergei Khrushchev reads a book entitled *A Welcome to U.S.A. Citizenship* as he waits to take the oath of allegiance to the United States to become a naturalized American citizen in 1999. Khrushchev is the son of former Soviet leader Nikita Khrushchev.

"I hereby declare, on oath, that I absolutely and entirely renounce and abjure all allegiance and fidelity to any foreign prince, potentate, state, or sovereignty, of whom or which I have heretofore been a subject or citizen; that I will support and defend the Constitution and laws of the United States of America against all enemies, foreign and domestic; that I will bear true faith and allegiance

Across the country every day, students recite the pledge of allegiance to the American flag. This convention began in the late 19th century, after a man named Francis Bellamy wrote the oath and began a campaign to make it a morning tradition in schools throughout the country.

to the same; that I will bear arms on behalf of the United States when required by the law; that I will perform noncombatant service in the armed forces of the United States when required by the law; that I will perform work of national importance under civilian direction when required by the law; and that I take this obligation freely without any mental reservation or purpose of evasion; so help me God.

By taking the oath, Donna now pledges her **allegiance** first and foremost to the United States. If Donna objected to the religious or military references in the oath, she could have still taken the oath but omitted those portions. After Donna took the oath, she and her family left as Jamaican-American citizens of the United States. ✶

A husband and wife pose with their children, who were adopted from Korea. The passage of the Child Citizenship Act, which went into effect in 2001, has made it easier for children adopted from other countries to become U.S. citizens.

Immigration to the
United States Today

On February 27, 2001, the Child Citizenship Act of 2000 went into effect. The act gave U.S. citizenship to children born outside the country if at least one parent is already a citizen. The child must be under 18, and it doesn't matter if the parent is a natural-born or naturalized citizen. For many American families adopting children from other countries, this was a great relief. It is estimated that 75,000 internationally adopted children have become citizens due to this act. Once the adoption is complete, the child is granted citizenship and all the rights and privileges that come with it.

The 2000 Census sets America's total population at more than 281 million people. Today's America is so diverse that the 2000 Census counted nearly 7 million people belonging to two, three, four, five, and even six ethnic races. Donna's children are among the 6.5 million people belonging to two ethnic groups.

In 2002, over 28 million people who had been born in another country now call the United States home. That's about 10 percent of the population. A census, like the one taken in 2000, indicates what areas of the world people are coming to America from. About 10 percent of the foreign-born population in America, like Donna, comes from the Caribbean. The 2000 Census also reports that nearly 35 percent of America's foreign-born population is from Central America,

49

CENSUS

The U.S. Constitution requires that a census, or count of the population, be taken every ten years. This is a costly and time-consuming project. Today, census information is collected by mail, the Internet, and through personal interviews.

The questions asked in a census change as the population changes. Information collected in a census includes age, sex, ethnic background, marital status, and income. The information is collected to let the government and its officials know who the citizens are in order to plan for beneficial public services, such as child-care centers, new roads and bridges, police and fire departments, elderly care, and schools. Businesses also use the information to plan for new factories, malls, and other services. In addition, the information is used to determine the number of seats a state gets in the House of Representatives and in the Electoral College. When a state gains or loses seats in the House or Electoral College, it is called reapportionment.

According to the Census information, in 2003 the population of the United States is projected at more than 285 million.

Information about the most recent U.S. Census can be found on the Internet at www.census.gov.

A form for the 2000 U.S. Census arrives at a Missouri mailbox. The census forms were sent to more than 120 million U.S. households. They were used to gather data for the census, which takes place every ten years. The information collected by census workers is used to determine what programs will receive funding and what areas of the country need legislative or financial attention.

Fifth grade students work together on a computer project at Claxton Elementary School in Asheville, North Carolina. Newer laws and programs are helping America become even more diverse.

about 25.5 percent is from Asia, a little over 15 percent is from Europe, nearly seven percent is from South America, and about eight percent is from other places, like Australia. Today, more than 35 percent of the foreign-born population has become naturalized United States citizens.

Just like today, foreign-born Americans made up 10 percent of the population in 1850. Where the census in 1850 differs from the one in 2000 is where the people are coming from. Back then, more people were coming from Europe than from anywhere else. The highest percentage came in 1910 when 15 percent of the population came from other countries. It is the continuous arrival of immigrants to America's shores that has made the United States the wonderful land of diversity that it is today. ✺

Chronology

25,000 B.C. The ancient ancestors of the Native Americans cross the Bering Strait and enter North America.

A.D. 1000 Viking explorer Leif Eriksson crosses the Atlantic Ocean and lands on the North American coast.

1492 Christopher Columbus sails into the Caribbean.

1501 Amerigo Vespucci sails to the "New World."

1526 Six hundred Spanish colonists and 100 African slaves arrive in North America.

1565 The Spanish colony of St. Augustine is established.

1598 Spanish settlers move into southwestern North America.

1604 French setters establish the Acadia colony in what is now Nova Scotia, Canada.

1606 English settlers arrive in what is now Virginia.

1607 English settlers establish the Jamestown colony.

1608 French setters establish the Quebec colony in what is now Canada.

1614 Dutch settlers establish New Netherlands (New York).

1619 African slaves arrive in Virginia colony.

1620 Pilgrims establish the Plymouth colony.

1626 Dutch settlers establish the city of New Amsterdam (New York City).

1630 Puritans establish the Massachusetts Bay colony.

1638 New Sweden is founded by the Swedish in what is now Delaware.

1654 Jewish settlers arrive in New Amsterdam.

1682 William Penn founds Pennsylvania.

1776 The United States declares its independence from Great Britain.

1780 Scottish immigrants arrive in America.

1787 The United States Constitution is written.

1789 Congress proposes 12 amendments to the Constitution.

1790 A two-year residence period before immigrants qualify for United States citizenship is enacted; French immigrants opposed to the French Revolution begin to arrive in the United States; the federal territory, Washington, D.C., is named the nation's capital.

1791 The states agree to 10 of the Constitutional Amendments (Bill of Rights).

1795 Congress raises the residency period to five years; the Eleventh Amendment is passed.

1798 The Alien and Sedition Acts raise the waiting period for citizenship to 14 years.

1804 Twelfth Amendment is passed.

1840 During the next 40 years, 37 million people immigrate to the United States.

1848 Chinese immigrants begin to arrive during the California Gold Rush.

1865 Thirteenth Amendment is passed.

1868 Fourteenth Amendment is passed.

1870 Fifteenth Amendment is passed.

1882 The Chinese Exclusion Act halts Chinese immigration as well as preventing criminals, people with diseases, and people likely to become dependent on public assistance from entering the country.

1885 The Alien Contract Labor Laws prohibit immigrants to work under contracts made prior to their arrival.

1886 The Statue of Liberty is erected in New York Harbor.

1891 The Immigration and Naturalization Service (INS) is created.

1892 Ellis Island is opened as an immigration-screening station.

1900 In the next 20 years, 10 million immigrants come to America.

1907 The United States and Japan reach an agreement whereby Japan would deny passports to Japanese laborers trying to enter the United States and the United States wouldn't enact laws stopping immigration from Japan.

1913 Sixteenth Amendment is passed; the Seventeenth Amendment is passed.

1917 The Immigration Act of 1917 further limits areas of the world from which people can immigrate to the United States.

1919 Eighteenth Amendment is passed.

1920 Nineteenth Amendment is passed.

1921 Congress establishes a quota system limiting the number of immigrants allowed in the country each year.

1924 The Immigration Act of 1924 further reduces the number of immigrants allowed in the United States each year.

1930 America enters the Great Depression.

1933 Twentieth Amendment is passed; the Twenty-first Amendment repeals the Eighteenth Amendment.

1941 Congress passes an act that refuses visas to immigrants whose presence in the United States might endanger public safety.

1943 Congress passes a bill allowing 105 Chinese immigrants into the United States each year.

1945 The War Brides Act gives visas to wives and children of men who served in the military.

1948- 1950 The Displaced Persons Act assists immigrants escaping persecution.

1950 The number of Mexican immigrants in the United States rises.

1951 Twenty-second Amendment is passed.

1952 Present-day naturalization methods are in effect.

1953 The Refugee Relief Act further assists immigrants escaping persecution.

1954 Ellis Island closes.

1961 Twenty-third Amendment is passed.

1964 Twenty-fourth Amendment is passed.

1965 The Immigration and Nationality Act limits the number of immigrants by hemisphere; Ellis Island is taken over by the National Park Service.

1967 Twenty-fifth Amendment is passed.

1971 Twenty-sixth Amendment is passed.

1974 The Home Rule Act establishes local elections in Washington, D.C.

1978 The Immigration and Nationality Act is amended, eliminating separate limits.

1980 The Refugee Act of 1980 reduces the worldwide limit and sets a limit of 50,000 for refugees.

1986 The Immigration Reform and Control Act penalizes employers hiring illegal immigrants.

1990 Immigration Act of 1990 sets the current limits for worldwide immigration to the United States; Ellis Island is re-opened as a museum.

1992 Twenty-seventh Amendment is passed.

1996 Illegal Immigration Reform and Immigrant Responsibility Act sets easier standards for deportation.

2000 The U.S. census is held throughout the country, finding that the population of the United States is more than 281 million.

2001 The Child Citizenship Act, which gives citizenship to children born outside of the United States who have at least one citizen parent, goes into effect in February.

2003 The populaton of the United States is estimated at more than 285 million.

Glossary

Allegiance to support, to be loyal to, or to devote to a cause, leader, or country.

Allied joined by compact or treaty.

Amend to add or alter in some way.

Bail security given for the release of a prisoner.

Ban a legal or formal prohibition.

Census official account of a population's age, race, sex, income, and occupation.

Deportation lawfully sending someone back to his or her native country.

Dictate to speak or read for a person to write down or for a machine to record.

Dictatorship a form of government in which all power is held by one person or a small group.

Famine an extreme scarcity of food.

Immune free from, exempt, protected.

Indentured sentenced to work for another for a specified amount of time.

Multiple sclerosis a disease that affects the nerves and muscles.

 58

Naturalize to undertake the process a person goes through to gain the rights and privileges of citizenship.

Persecution the act of harassing someone because of their beliefs.

Poll tax a tax of a fixed amount per person.

Preferential showing preference for.

Quota a number limit given to determine the amount of people allowed to immigrate to a country.

Self-incrimination the act of exposing oneself to prosecution.

Unconstitutional not according to or consistent with the constitution of a nation.

Vacancy an empty space.

Visa an official stamp on a passport allowing entry into the country giving the stamp.

Further Reading

Books

Alesi, Gladys. *How to Prepare for the U.S. Citizenship Test*. New York: Barron's Educational Series, 2000.

Freedman, Russell. *Immigrant Kids*. New York: Econo-Clad Books, 1999.

Kosof, Anna. *Living in Two Worlds*. New York: Twenty-First Century Books, 1996.

Lawlor, Veronica. *I Was Dreaming of Coming to America: Memories from the Ellis Island Oral History Project*. New York: Viking Children's Books, 1995.

Polacco, Patricia. *The Keeping Quilt*. New York: Simon & Schuster, 1998.

Internet Resources

http://www.census.gov

The Web site for the U.S. Census Bureau, providing extensive census information on a wide variety of topics.

http://www.ellisisland.org

This Web site is devoted to the history of Ellis Island and the immigrants who came through its doors.

http://www.ins.usdoj.gov

The Immigration and Naturalization Service Web site provides information on becoming a citizen, one's rights and responsibilities, as well as forms, fees, and other information.

http://www.nara.gov

This is the National Archives and Records Administration Web site, providing a place where people can conduct research, look up family members, and read about various laws—all online.

http://www.firstgov.gov

This Web site provides a tremendous amount of information on the United States government, its bodies and how they work, as well as a breakdown of the government by topic.

Index

Photo Credits

Contributors

Barry Moreno has been librarian and historian at the Ellis Island Immigration Museum and the Statue of Liberty National Monument since 1988. He is the author of *The Statue of Liberty Encyclopedia,* which was published by Simon & Schuster in October 2000. He is a native of Los Angeles, California. After graduation from California State University at Los Angeles, where he earned a degree in history, he joined the National Park Service as a seasonal park ranger at the Statue of Liberty; he eventually became the monument's librarian. In his spare time, Barry enjoys reading, writing, and studying foreign languages and grammar. His biography has been included in *Who's Who Among Hispanic Americans, The Directory of National Park Service Historians, Who's Who in America,* and *The Directory of American Scholars.*

Rob Maury is currently working for a national magazine. His material has appeared in newspapers and on the Internet. He lives with his family in Hatfield, Pennsylvania.